I Am Like An Elephant!

by Isabel Thomas

All About Elephants

An African elephant is the biggest land animal.

An elephant's toe is bigger than your hand!

Elephants are very strong.

This elephant grabs a branch with his trunk.

Lots of living things are like elephants in some way. Let's see which ones!

A Shrew

It's an elephant shrew. It looks like a mouse with a little trunk!

Elephant shrews eat insects. A long snout helps them hunt. It has long whiskers, too.

A Shark

This is an elephant shark. It has a long snout. The snout looks like a garden **hoe**.

Elephant sharks dig with their snout. They dig up shellfish from the **seabed**.

A Serpent

This is an elephant trunk serpent. It's an **aquatic** animal.

Its skin is crinkled like an elephant's skin. This helps it to swim well.

A Caterpillar

It's an elephant hawk caterpillar. It looks like an elephant's trunk!

This moth grew from the caterpillar. It is not like an elephant. Elephants are not pink and green!

A Beetle

This is an elephant beetle. It's one of the biggest beetles.

Elephant beetles have horns for whacking **foes**.

A Seal

It's an elephant seal. It looks like it has a trunk.

This elephant seal blew bubbles in the water!

A Bird

This is an elephant bird. Elephant birds had crinkled skin on their legs. They are now **extinct**.

Elephant birds never flew. They ran on their tiptoes!

A Plant

This is an elephant ear plant. It grows in damp soil.

People grow elephant ears as houseplants. They need lots of water.

I Am Like An Elephant!

This is an ant. Ants are little but very strong.

Lots of living things are like elephants. Can you list them all?

Look It Up

aquatic: living in water

extinct: no longer living

foes: people or animals that battle

hoe: a garden tool to dig up weeds

seabed: the bottom of the sea

Index